Busy Buzzing Bumblebees

and Other Tongue Twisters

Alvin Schwartz · illustrated by Paul Meisel

🔥 HarperTrophy®

A Division of HarperCollinsPublishers

HarperCollins®, �055®, Harper Trophy®, and I Can Read Book®
are trademarks of HarperCollins Publishers Inc.

Busy Buzzing Bumblebees and Other Tongue Twisters
Text copyright © 1982 by Alvin Schwartz
Illustrations copyright © 1992 by Paul Meisel
Printed in the U.S.A. All rights reserved.
Newly Illustrated Edition
Published in hardcover by HarperCollins Publishers.

Library of Congress Cataloging-in-Publication Data
Schwartz, Alvin, date
   Busy buzzing bumblebees and other tongue twisters / by Alvin
Schwartz ; illustrated by Paul Meisel.
      p.   cm. — (An I can read book)
   Summary: A collection of forty-six tongue twisters.
   ISBN 0-06-444036-2 (pbk.)
   [1. Tongue twisters. [1. Tongue twisters.]   I. Meisel, Paul,
ill.   II. Title   III. Series.
[PN6371.5.S38   1992b]   91-4800
818'.5402—dc20   CIP
                                                         AC

New Harper Trophy edition, 1992.

For Barbara, Betsy, and Nan
—A.S.
For Andrew
—P. M.

A tongue twister

will twist your tongue

and make you laugh.

Just say it three times

as fast as you can.

Flash message!

Six sharp smart sharks!

6

Swim, Sam! Swim, Sam! Swim, Sam!

Well swum, Sam!

Six sticky sucker sticks.

9

Eight gray geese.

Nine nice night nurses nursing nicely.

Sixty-six

sneaky snakes.

13

Tom Knott knits
knitted knotted knots.

14

If Stu chews shoes,
should Stu choose
the shoes he chews?

15

Big Bill blew

big blue bubbles.

16

Down the slippery slide

slid Sam.

Which witch watched which watch?

She sells seashells

by the seashore.

20

The black back brake broke.

Danger!

Deep damp dark

dirty deadly dismal dungeon!

23

To toot and to hoot!

To hoot and to toot!

Ruth's wet red roof.

Polly Pobble's

pot of pebbles.

Blue booties

are beauties.

A proper copper coffeepot.

Tillie's twin thin sister.

Big Ben Blimber.

Shy sly Sheila.

Sam Short thought

Sara Smith so sweet.

Nellie Needle nibbles noodles.

Peter pared the peel

from the pile of pears

in the pail.

Ron rolled a round roll
around a round room.

38

Crispy crusty crunchy crunch.

"This bun is better buttered,"
Billy muttered.

Blake the baker
bakes black bread.

41

Pete's pop shops

for chops

in chop shops.

Cheap sheep soup.

Fresh fruit float.

45

The big book crook

took the big cookbook.

47

On a light night,

I don't need

a night-light.

Did the butterfly
flutter by
the butterfly?

50

Five fat frogs fled from

fifty fierce fish.

A big black bug

bit a big black bear.

Crickets chirp in thickets.

There is a spider

inside the cider

beside her.

Busy buzzing bumblebees

buzzing busily.

A picky pet pig

picked a pine pigpen.

Hiccup teacup.

When you have the hiccups,

take a breath,

and try this twister.

And your hiccups may go away.

59

How high would

a horsefly fly

if a horsefly

would fly high?

How much dew
would a dewdrop drop,
if a dewdrop did drop dew?

Crow, Cock!

Caw, Crow!

People all over the world use tongue twisters. They tell them in French and Chinese and all the other languages.

Some of these twisters are very old. The famous "Peter Piper picked a peck of pickled peppers" twister and others started out in England over three hundred years ago.

But there also are twisters that are brand-new, like "Crispy crusty crunchy crunch" and "Cheap sheep soup." It is fun to make them up.

You can make up a twister of your own. Just think of a sentence in which all the words start with the same letter or sound. And you will twist a tongue.